BUSY MURALS

Maiche Lev

BUSY MURALS

by Maiche Lev
All Rights Reserved
Copyright © 2020 HDW Publications

Cover and book design by David Bricker

ISBN:978-0-9975757-4-3

http://www.maichelev.com

Contents

BUSY MURALS

Longer Boats

Longer boats are coming to win us
They're coming to win us
They're coming to win us
Longer boats are coming to win us
Hold on to the shore
They'll be taking the key from the door

— Yusuf Islam

Dedication

This book is dedicated to the grand NPR gals, Terry Gross and Dianne Rheme. How many afternoons have you made so worthwhile?

And of course, Marian McPartland. You were all about the music — straight-ahead piano jazz — an English gal with the boogie-woogie — a master.

Okay, Ira. *This American Life.* You still ring the bell, buddy.

And that Krista Tippett, you minx. *I can't stand it!*

And God! This book is also dedicated to the memory of Cokie Roberts, a pioneer. What she was made of — New Orleans's first one little true dreamer — is still there for me and you.

Miss Woodruff and Desjardins and Yamiche: We got the makings of a band here, girls.

Letter to the Editor

My editor
Dave Bricker
He and I rode out the corona pandemic
On the phone
Processing this selection of poems
Which I've chosen to entitle, *Busy Murals*

If becoming tired and bored with yourself
Is a dilemma of the irresolute
Having published six books of poetry since 2014
The ongoing activity of publishing more
Was a prospect a little stuck

About two-and-a-half weeks into the pandemic
The whole world was getting cabin fever
I called David and he suggested we start working
    by phone…
And so we did
It's a game changer
To have something to work toward in your week
Having to bypass our 8:00 a.m. breakfasts at the
    Bagel Emporium
We reconnected and got down to work

I decided to go more neutral-to-positive with this collection
More civil

And parabolic
Less gripe-strewn
This book is kind of like a...
A set of keys you find behind the treasure chest in the
    fish tank...
After you just replaced them all!

How in the...?

Bricker and I worked in ninety-minute sessions
Like ping-pong champs letting loose
In a little more than six weeks
We had this book of poems down
Well ... maybe it was more like nine

I was repeatedly reminded
Of how fortunate I am
To have so professional a literarian available to me
And in six years he hasn't upped his rates
The familiarity of our experience reading together
Was just as it has always been between us
Even-handed and fluid...
And quite a hoot!

It's funny...
David and I grew up in the same kindergarten
He was a little older than me...
In the next group

So I'm sure I dug up things in the sandbox
He'd buried the day before
I love that

And you know what the piano man Billy Joel said
About the piano man Elton John
On one of their tours together?
"He's much better than me, man!"

Mister Bricker would no doubt like to tell you
That *Busy Murals* has made-up words, made-up spellings,
    made-up facts
And other cockamamie stuff you can't punctuate
And probably don't need in the first place…
In spite of his protests

And furthermore…
All of this pandemic lockdown
Is for prior-suffering germophobes
The mother lode jackpot
A lottery number come in
Respectfully…
He and the wife love English television so much
And now they have time to watch it all

And so, Mr. Bricker
I'm all oatmealed up
And my coffee's hot

8 — Maiche Lev

Who's to say ten o'clock isn't too early to rock 'n' roll?

Morning, Maiche…

Whaddaya got for me today?

—July, 2020

Good

Good
Good enough
Good gracious
Good heavens
Good stuff
Good stuff, man
Good Golly, Miss Molly
Hey, good lookin'
Good as I been to you…
Good grades are important, but not everything
Is that a goodly way of goin' about things?
The goods
The Browns are pretty good this year
No one from 'round here ever come to no good
Y' good?
She done me…
She done me good

Try the casserole with peas
It's a little show-offy but it's good
How was the movie?
Good … but not great
You're not missing anything
She's too good for him

A good man is hard to find
"Well, good reader…"
Do you think we can make things good again?
I don't give a good goddam anymore
Johnny B. Goode tonight, yeah
I say go … Go Johnny!
Johnny B. Goode
She's good around the eyes
Goody two-shoes
Goody-goody
Good 'n' plenty
Mr. Goodbar
Congratulations! Y' got a good deal
How good you must feel
Why you goodfornothin…!

There's a place to stay but it's a good ways up the road from
    here…
Good strawberries this year, hon
The Cape of Good Hope
Good crowd tonight
Good lovin'
Good vittles
Mmmm, curry!
Good odds
Good angles
Good attitude
I been in a good way lately

Good headspace
Good head shop
Good luck with that!

Good haircut
A good hair day
Good babysitter
Good coffee
Good help
Good guac ... *mmmmm*
Good beach access
G' day, mate!
Good call
Michaelangelo's is more than good frozen food
And Tabatchnik's
Wendy's always had a good salad bar
I hope you have a good reason for this
Good sound system!
Tonight's gonna be a good night
Keep singing; you were always so good

You're no good
You're no good
You're no good
Baby...
Good luck!
Don't y' know that goodbye doesn't mean forever?
It doesn't?

Goodbye is too good a word
Good roommates always…
Have chronic…

Good public transportation
Good motto
Good theme song
Gooden pitched for the Yanks
What was his number?
You're too good to me
A good sushi place
It's good to see your smilin' face tonight
Good God, y'all!
Good things to know about adopting rescue animals
Good pay
Well, some people ain't no damn good
Y' can't trust 'em
Y' can't love 'em
Your opinion means nothin!
Life is good
God is good
All the hippies in the Grateful Dead parking lot say,
   "Have a good show"
The greater good
Good sex requires concentration
Good riddance
Good-time Charlie

Good intentions can be evil

Good afternoon

Welcome to Galaxy Bar and Grill

Muddy Waters said

If it's good to ya

Mus' be good fo' ya

He's had it good

Now the sonovabitch wants it better

His shit was questionable but pretty good …

Which ain't saying much

Have a good week

Have a good one

Is there a good place for me to get sick in?

Good website

Always good gumbo at the St. Charles Tavern

Good résumé

Good sense of rhythm

Good judgement

Good 'n' drunk

Good SNL cast this year

Good salsa

Good pancakes

Cool motorcycle!

Yeah … It's a Suzuki GS-500

Good way to get yourself killed

A good bit of doctoring

Good evening Mr. and Mrs. America
From border to border and coast to coast
And all the ships at sea

Muzak, Oh Muzak

Some music tries to scare you
An assault of pentagraphoric chords from Dorito-breath hell
In the moment it's so *big*
Its laughable

"Smoke on the Water" is sacred ground, I understand
And Ozzy *rules...*
Yeah, somewhere out there...
Around a puddle on a piss planet
You there with your bad self...
You can buy a "Kiss" coffin

Yeah ... *you* can

What twelve-year-old soul singers have to offer...

Phoebe Snow's heart's in heaven
It sprawls the aurora borealis of 140 universes...
And only twenty-eight ever been discovered!

And how Roberta Flack will be received...
The natural singers
For the love of Clydie King on high
What ease caress the angel's rise

Praise be!

What Are You Doing?

Ever notice that the pool's too cold?

The sun's too hot?

The grass is all dry?

And the rain's too hard?

Money

One Koch brother turned to the other Koch brother
   and said…

"If you don't give me your Pixie Sticks…
I'm tellin' Mom you pee in the dandelions!"

At the Light

When I see a car with a "Make America Great Again"
    bumper sticker
I drive up beside them…
And just *look*

You Can't Always Get What You Want

Is the Rolling Stones song, "You Can't Always Get What You Want" public property, having been recorded and published more than forty years ago?

Or did Mick and the boys make such a questionable choice of endorsement?

Unplugged (But then Again)

All these singing contests on TV
Like some kind of *poison*
I wonder…
Will people even enjoy their voices in the shower anymore?

But then again…
Maybe these shows give people
The spirit to take the chance to emote
To *throw* the voice
To *belt* it out

It's like the X-Box Guitar Hero
You could say it's a bastard — and it *is!*
But then again…
Some of those hundreds of thousands of kids
Will graduate to real guitars
And that's a good thing…

One should never say, "I can't sing"
One should never say, "I can't dance"

And the traffic lights turn blue tomorrow…[1]

---

1 Hendrix, Jimmy, "The Wind Cries Mary" *Are You Experienced?* Reprise, 1967

Kavanaugh
(Maiche Lev with D. Bricker)

Yes, I was once a teenager |Beer was important | We were that young and that rowdy | And that drunk | We'd all seen *Animal House and felt like we had to live up to that* | *A girl was a thing* | All of our big brothers had *Playboy* and worse| And I'm sorry for whatever got ugly | This doctor testifying to my antics | Well, that was one American neighborhood… | A dime a dozen | I'm embarrassed | You win | I'm humiliated in front of my family and my country

I have read half a library of legal books | I have applied my heart and soul | Cover to cover | I love the law | I understand and recognize the long-standing implications of party politics | My impartiality is a sworn obligation | So stated | Here and now | What will be from my chair?

This trial | This hearing | This humiliating exposé… | It isn't enough for me to say, "Boys will be boys" | But that's what it was back then | And maybe for a little too long

I am a father | And a husband | And a lawyer of forty years | A man experienced | Ready to serve in this country's highest court | Faithfully apologizing | Faithfully adherent

— Kavanaugh

From Chaplin

Tarpon and jack are not good eatin' fish
All bones
But with half a palm of sea salt
They make alright soup
Right, Charlie?

Merchant Marines

Merchant marine families do alright
Two-bedroom places
Carpeted
Like-new appliances
A pool in the village
Daddy's gone for months at a time, though
The adolescent boy is in with the boys
As is the girl who had another abortion last year

The transmission in the minivan is shot
Then there's the kids' trip to Washington
Phone bills
Electric bills
Water bills
Christmas
Co-pays
Winter coats
Sporting goods
Summer camp
Braces
Entertainment
The unexpected
Taxes and…

Merchant marine families do alright

Cuties

Y' can't buy Cuties tofu mini ice-cream sandwiches
Because that's what the people were buying
In the big mainstream supermarkets
Not the rest of the big sugar confections
On display door-to-door
Business
Big business
Think I'll write the president

The "how of the cow"
The "how of the cow," Sir!
It walks
It talks
It's full of chalk
The lactate fluid extracted from the female of the bovine
    species is highly prolific
To the nth degree!

And *that* is the "how of the cow," Sir!

Colostrum

For nine months — nine — she slaved in rice paddies
For nine months — nine — she bent over cotton buds
For nine months — nine — she worked on an assembly line
   in a factory
For nine months — nine — she suffered in sweat shops
   in the city

For nine months — nine — she ran a busy company
For nine months — nine — she ran around a medical office
For nine months — nine — she took care of her family
For nine months — nine — something kicked and pawed
   inside her

So of the 328.2-million people on the North American
   continent
How few of us know what "colostrum" is?
She blooms…

Mister

Colonel Behrani (House of Sand and Fog)

Colonel Behrani said to his son
"Americans don't deserve what they have
They have the eyes of small children
Who are forever looking for the next source of destruction
Entertainment
And sweet taste in the mouth"

Jail

I'm glad I'm not in jail
They keep it *cold* in there
Time
Time in a cage
Clanging doors clang like crashing cars colliding
I'm lying on this bed
On this bed I'm always lying
On this bed
I'm always lying on this bed

The sound of two-hundred men in 12 x 7-foot cells is
   a rookery
A house in a storm
Pelted by debris
And it keeps up
Never goes away
No privacy
And eventually…
They come for you
What d' they want with me?
Jail
Glad I'm not in jail

Jail
Prison
The penitentiary

I was in for eighteen hours once
That was enough for me
Daddy come to get me
A misdemeanor in the fourth degree
Unloading drums in a handicapped spot
At 3:00 AM
South Beach
The first cell was clean
I walked in circles
Singing all the songs I knew from memory

I remember clearly
They moved us around across Miami
At dawn we were in a chain-link fence corral
The prostitutes arrested the night before were in the next
In their apparel
Eventually we were in a place with a few telephones
Y' get a paper bag with a baloney sandwich
And you're glad for it

Tall guards in green jumpsuits
Beat a loudmouth making trouble…
With billy clubs
Bad moments
Baloney sandwich

The Department of Corrections
How many times y' been in here, Whitey?

How many times for you, Chico?
Hommes, I don't know…

Jail
A cage for a human being
People put away
They've done wrong
Done wrong again
Can't be trusted not to hurt others
They're in … "rehabilitation"

All I did was break in and steal
Yeah, I tied them up but I didn't lay a hand on 'em, Judge
We only wanted t' scare 'em

Jail
I sold drugs
That's all I know, your honor
That's my money maker
My in
"That's three strikes, felon"

Jail
Your honor
Yes, she was underage but I didn't know
She didn't look thirteen
She didn't act thirteen
Your honor…

Jail
Like a rap sheet
The scenarios reach down to the floor
The extreme mentality of the ghetto dweller
Gangsta rap is its own powder keg

I told myself I should read a few books about the
    prison system
And then start writing...
And not before
But I had these two sheets of paper...
With the heading, "I'm glad I'm not in Jail"
Doesn't feel like I've written anything that says that much

Dade...
No one got ahold of me
But I'm sure it happens
A quick ass-kickin' for fun on the white boy
Inside...
I thought of thrd-world jails as a living nightmare

*The degree of civilization in a society can be judged by entering
    its prisons.*

                                    —Fyodor Dostoevsky

400 Miles

I will walk 400 miles
T' see my mama 'n' my papa 'n' my sister
Yeah … 400 miles
T' see my brother, the Doctor Mister

I will walk 400 miles
Along familiar shores
400 miles
I'll be wonderin' what I'm walkin' for

400 miles
twenty miles times twenty days
400 miles
Florida salty summer haze
It's gonna seem like a long, long climb
One day at a time
One day at a time

400 miles
I won't carry any dead weight
I won't hold a sign
I'll go barefoot on the sand
With my sandals strapped to my behind

Oh, 400 miles
Ain't nobody but my cats gonna miss me

Shoot, I'd be liable to stay right here in town
If my dental hygienist would only come on just once and
   kiss me

400 miles
Godspeed in slow motion
Gonna walk all night
Don't need any suntan lotion

400 miles
By the ocean side
A1A must've gone somewhere to hide
400 miles
That should be enough
400 miles
It's gonna be rough

400 miles
Prob'ly take a Greyhound home
I'll be the guy next to you there
Starin' out the window

400 miles
Too hot to think of broken love
400 miles
A drifter in a beat-up motel bathtub

400 miles
Armadillo, possum
Turtle, hare, snake, raccoon
Redfish, flounder, jack, snook
Catch tarpon all afternoon

400 miles
Windblown
Down and dusty
Holes in my shirt and the knees of my jeans
Look at that dude
Down to his last dungarees

400 miles
No, really…
Be a banjo 'cross my knee
How many times can one poor soul sing
"The Rose of Alabamee?"

Oh brown Rosie
Rose of Alabama
Sweet tobacco posey
Ta-loo-rah-loo-rah-lay
Rosie!

400 miles
Wish I had a dog

Wish I walked around the block a few times
Says this certifiable bump on a log

400 miles is what 400 miles is for
In 400 miles, I'll be knockin' on someone's door...
400 miles is what 400 miles is for...

Wish me luck—I'm going in!
Hope I don't lose my sense of humor!

You Finish it

When boys are small
They play cops and robbers
Cowboys and Indians
Or War
The Action Adventure Channel

When girls are small
They play with dolls in doll houses
Lipstick
Dress shoes
Sunglasses
The Home Shopping Channel

Now *you* finish it

TV America

It's got the car chase
The foot chase
Gritty David Chase
Got the fighting
Hand-to-hand combat
Rock 'em sock 'em
Knife fight
Gun fight
Machine Gun Kelly
"You're one cold-hearted sonofabitch, Wyatt Earp"
Rocky Balboa's egg-drop burp
Got the black with the black
The white with the white
One sexy teen
And one roly-poly fat kid
Freestyle rap
How he wears his pants
And how he wears his hat
My grown kid can sing the Prince of Bel Aire song in
    his sleep
Of course, thay *all* can
My elder sister can gather herself and sing The Partridge
    Family's "I think I Love You" amazingly well
And Webster...
I never did quite get that...
Not that I tried

Where did the Olson twins go?

The Clash recorded "Pirate Radio"

Just think of *Three's Company*

We sat there watching…

Poor Jack!

9-0-2-1-4-7-8

The kids won't eat and the dog can't sleep

And then the day came when you could order your
  own movie

And nudity!

Look… there's 600 categories

Little House on the Prairie

Hoss, himself

Who shot J.R. anyway, man?

It's got…

Talk shows

Who's your favorite…?

Michael Douglas or Merv Griffin?

I guess Oprah Winfrey did a world of good compared
  to Springer

Who still has 'em all eating out of his hand

Did you know that Ellen DeGeneres is a really good
  softball player?

It's got…

Look … I got a TV in my telephone

A TV in my telephone!

Hello Moto

It's got news … and religion … politics … pornography

Grandma left her last cent to a billy-goat named
  Robert Tilton

He was speaking in tongues

Outside the walls of Jerusalem

And you know…

After inheriting grandma's $2.4 million

He didn't even send a letter of appreciation

No offense, Mr. Tilton!

American TV has goblins and gladiators

Dungeons

Dragons

The Wonderful World of Disney

Brought to you by Nabisco

Mutual of Omaha

No one knows who Marlin Perkins was anymore!

That's what a Land Rover is

Alcoa…

Alcoa can't wait!

It's got charities

Telethons

Jerry Lewis was a beautiful man, wasn't he?

The French *die* for him

The Concert for Bangladesh way back when

FEMA

OXFAM

Live Aid

Farm Aid

Disaster Relief

It's got the Superbowl
It's got the Superbowl halftime show!
The Superbowl commercials
Thanks, Mean Joe!
It's got exercise in leotards at six-thirty in the morning
Weather girls…
Sure are sexy at 7:00 a.m.
Al Roper had a double-beef cheeseburger thrown at him
It's got cheap advertising campaigns in high rotation
I had to change the station!
Howard Cosell … messing with Mohammed Ali's head
Who's Mad Jack?
And for that matter, who was Ben?
I am Ben
I smoke Chesterfields
Doesn't seem to be any kind of problem
Firestone tires…
Seven wrapped in three … sealed in one!
J-Lo used to date a handsome man from Boston
But she married an ugly little runt like me
Name's Mark Anthony
I saw him last night
At the Paul Simon & Friends Celebration on channel…
It was late in the evening
And he was as good as any of 'em

What a voice, man!
What moves!

¡Qué carisma genuino!
I might go out and buy an album!

American TV
American Television

Jane, Get me off this crazy thing!

I Should Read More

I would read more
But if I'm not capturing something of my own to grasp
To define
To conjure
It sits on the tip of my tongue
Runs around the scope of my mind…
An original thought
A revelation

And I get excited by what other people call "plagiarism"
As anyone who's read me can tell
I say to those detractors
"Go ask the original artists—
Dylan or Springsteen or the Petty camp
Or Gordon Lightfoot or John Hiatt
Ask them if they feel I've served them well"

When I'm writing
And something from Warren Zevon's "Bad Luck Streak in
    Dancing School" fits
Well, yeah…
I inhaled it back then
And now I'm riding it all the way home

Their world
Your world

My world
Our world
The world

On a related note…
Sometimes now …
If I'm half-asleep
And some beautifully sad piece of music comes over the radio
I find myself having to get up unreservedly
To turn it off
Anything deeply heart-wrenching…
Bars going up around me
Tentacles reaching in…
It's like that

I remember twenty-five years ago
Jill, my wife-to-be, refused from me
A copy of Mark Knopfler's soundtrack to the movie Cal
"David, I love it
But I won't listen to it
It's so sad…"

I guess these days I'm learning
That sadness is its own deconstruct

So...

I don't know exactly where I'm going with this page...

Maybe I just need a big dog...

Or two

My Newest Latest Smallest

My newest latest smallest artistic endeavor to be…
Hitting all the thrift shops in Florida
For their used Matchbox Hot Wheels cars
There's always an odd box in some musty corner
And a decrepit old white woman
With the good stuff around her desk
In the center-block establishment
Probably built back in the 1920s
Its roof somehow original

I'll stop in in my cycling shorts and enjoy the place
And I'll walk out with a fat bag
Full of those marked-up, scratched-up miniatures
That we were all so hypnotized by

Then I'll go to the post office
And send them to my place down south
By the time I get back from my ride
I'll have a *mound* of pre-owned Hot Wheels
To make a busy mural out of

Fun!
Elmers fun!
I think I still got half a gallon

My newest latest smallest

Man!

He can lay a driveway flat
Level
Long
Flush…
Hard hat
Caterpillar
Cat

He can install a window frame
Without a scratch
Cut the drywall
Run the sockets
Grout
Wet
Sponge
Patch

He's got a measuring tape and a ruler
And a rolling wheel that clicks as it counts
Before the cement sets
Spread the excess if any mounts

His hands haven't been countin' money
Or pushin' a pencil or pen
His hands are like mitts

He's not into skinny
He likes some meat on his women

He can wire a house for electricity
He can run water lines
Cut tile
He can paint a whole house without a run or a drip
Yes, siree
Hardwood floors
Doorbells
New front doors
He's got the Home Depot man's friendly smile

Man!
The whole nine yards
A banana tree
Got a green Thumb
Royal Palm
Bougainvillea
In purple…
And red raspberry

A bass boat
Hunting gear
A rifle with a scope
They asked me, "Ron, you wanna go?"

I said, "Uh… nope
It's too goddamn cold
The ground's too hard
And I don't get up that early
For anyone or anything…
Ever!"

I'm no boy scout
But I'm glad you are
I been eatin' all your beef jerky
Have fun in your lean-to
Hope y' don't get bum-rushed by a moose
Have fun
Bring us two-hundred pounds of venison
Say hello to Smokey
Don't forget your snake-bite kit

And someone always forgets his boots

Tropical Exposure, Exposure Tropicale

You're up!
Sitting there
Hit the light
Take your shower
Get dressed
Have a puff and a cup
And you're gone

Tropical Exposure
Exposure Tropicale

You're up!
Sitting there
Hit the light
Take your shower
Get dressed
Have a puff and a cup
Before dawn

Tropical Exposure
Exposure Tropicale

In four-and-a-half hours that alarm is gonna ring
Four-and-a-half hours ain't enough time to put it all down
To get up 'n' get it all goin'

Tropical Exposure
Exposure Tropicale

Four-and-a-half hours ain't spring flowers
Though y' feel better after your shower
This terrycloth towel
This terrycloth robe
The news is on the TV
No … the news is on National Public Radio

Coffee's brewed and waitin'
I may not know how to use my phone
But I'm *down* with the coffee machine

Tropical Exposure
Exposure Tropicale

I got two Portuguese water dogs
And a black-and-tan Louisiana hound named Vedder
My day starts out special, man
And jus' keeps getting' better

Tropical Exposure
Exposure Tropicale

The sun comes up
Papers are delivered

The water is warmer than the air
The school bus comes
The boulevard runs
Those aren't garbage men
The life of a civil sanitation engineer

Don't let a whole year go by
Before gettin' in your community pool
I had one right across the street from my front door
Didn't make it in once all year
Ever feel like a fool?
I swear it was a stone's throw away
From where I sat and smoked and smoked
And fucking smoked!

Tropical Exposure
Exposure Tropicale

Day or night
Walk down this street
In this sticky heat
You'll hear trumpets and bongos
Drums and guitars
And all kinds o' song
Everybody feels so good
And for a while there
Aren't We All Just Gettin' Along?

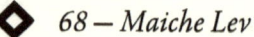

68 — *Maiche Lev*

Tropical Exposure

Exposure Tropicale

Nurses

You don't know how hard nurses work
Until you've landed in the hospital
For a couple of days
And witnessed one
At the end of a twelve-to-sixteen-hour shift
Having to shoulder and push off your room's doorway
To gain a step into the ward's busy hall
In those sturdy shoes
Creased by the weight and hours
Of another day's pressing on

"Don't you ever go home?"

Face Dances (Ryazantseza)

Alina…
R-E-V-Z-E-S-V-A-T-N-A…
That's not it…
R-E-Z-N-A-V-Z-T-N-A-V…
No … that's not it, either…
R-E-S-N-A-B-N-O-V-L-E-V
Wrong!
R-E-S-L-A-V-N-A-S-E-V
Nope…
R-E-H-Z-N-I-S-L-A-V-E-V
Not even close!
R-E-Z-N-O-V-N-A-L-A-V
I'll never get it…

Alina … her name is music
Poetry
Power

R-E-S-N-A-V-S-A-T-L-A-V
Why even try?
R-A-S-N-A-V-L-I-N-A-V
Enough … forget it!
R-A-Z-N-A-V-L-S-N-A-V
Oh, please!
I'm not into your passport picture
I just like your nose

The Greyhound Experience

Sit toward the front
No matter what
Or you will have the scent of blue latrine pellets
In your sinuses well into the next day

It's usually too cold or too hot in the coach
So travel in undershirt and sweatshirt
Layer

The driver stays awake at 73° night or day.
A light blanket keeps you warm and isolated
Untouched

The seats *usually* recline
I have been on a bus
    Loaded to capacity
In a seat with the air conditioner
Dripping constantly on my head
God!

A neck pillow costs a little less than $20
You forget it at the next stop's departure
But ya don't care because it was pretty grimy
From your own sweat or drool

The drivers can be mean, vindictive, or overbearing
They give their speech about headphones
Being turned down
Speaking too loud
The use of profanity and smoking
Using alcohol or *any* drugs
All of which lead to expulsion from the coach
Tar and feathering
I always vape under my blanket

Vindictive…
I have seen people in the wee hours
Get handed their luggage from under the bay
And left at the next town's crappy depot
Dejected but lighting up!

Yeah man,
People still smoke
It's a lower middle-class thing…

So is Greyhound, come to think of it
Sneaking a puff in the evil commode
Can get you a long, long night in Lake City
And these people don't have money for a $125 motel room
Or even a $75 Motel Six
Vindictiveness…
Power…

Authority….
Some drivers can be cruel…

Sleeping on a droning Greyhound Bus
Is as comfortable as being in King Kong's mother's womb
Only, she's sitting upright
With the root of a great cypress trunk digging into her ribs

Who farted?
Everyone did
Twice
America loves barbeque

Who's snoring?
Everyone is
It's not that bad…
Unless it is

Fact:
Every 400 miles
These great blue whales are refueled
And emptied for cleaning
Now hold on to your ticket!
Don't lose your ticket!

Every type of personality in those seats
Some are long-term addicts

Just out of rehab or out of jail
Who tend to talk in expletives
And sad, short bursts of speech that make sense only
   to themselves

Best conversations you'll ever have in your life
Can come from strangers
Whose background is the polar opposite of your own

Just last week
I sat from Orlando to Pensacola
With a woman about my age who stood about 4' 9" tall
She had just come out of rehab for the fourth or fifth time
(Like me in my twenties)
A raging alcoholic
Looked a lot like Rene Zellweger
We spoke in hushed tones for two full hours in the dark
Before the ride was up
I gave her half a pack of cigarettes
Twenty bucks
And a copy of one of my books
I asked her at least forty questions
And I learned about her impoverished life in Tennessee
Her four children
Two of them, autistic
She told me stories in a voice so true
She cried from the heart once or twice, choking back tears

W shared two little yogurt packs with plastic spoons
Her hair curly and graying…
Kelly
She could've stepped off "Cold Mountain"
Greyhound
America…

One time
Crossing North Florida
I failed to bring a sweatshirt
So cold I put my arms inside my tee-shirt to stay warm
Like kids do

An elderly black woman seated next to me
Removed half her shawl—a talisman
And invited me to share its warmth
We practically snuggled
So kind
Our shoulders touching
The temperature on the dashboard read 71°
(That's almost as cold as jail)
I could sense this woman was a church-goer
I could've been anyone
And she threw me a line

Personalities…
All with telephones

What did humanity do without Samsung?
In the seat left and right and behind
Y' hear the same profanity
Nigga this
Nigga that
Or sad Southern Meth monster types
In a drawl of unfortunate woe

Or sometimes something else entirely…
Herbalife reps
Foreign languages
An irrepressible burst of laughter
A New *Yawker*
A young ex-con
You know, an American gumbo
Fifty-some comfortable seats
Tempered glass windows,
Air-conditioned
Sixty-five miles-per-hour

At layovers
Which are usually less than a few hours long
You don't hang out outside the walls of the terminal much at
    all
Greyhound stations,
Most of the larger ones at least
Have security

But these tiled "obelisks" are commonly the jumpin'est open
    place in those towns
So, look out!

Do not leave your bags unattended
Inside or outside
If you're hankering for a smoke
Or want to find the nearest place with at least a few
    cellophane-wrapped apples
Well, the bus depot has a lit exterior
And to its light comes that which is attracted to light…
Beware of the troubled
Stay in the ark
You become a potential victim
As soon as you step through the exit
And … your bags are like fumbled footballs
Christmas presents…
Get it?
One talks to you while the other swipes
One talks to you while the other with a blackjack
    approaches
Bad
And worse
It's the same anywhere
Late at night in dipshit towns
Orlando
Fort Pierce

Ocala
Tallahassee
Panama City
You're a target.
Vipers who've lost all ray of hope
"Got a smoke?"

Once on a Greyhound Bus
The overhead rack a few rows up was squeaking
Badly
And it was getting to me
Deeply
I turned my headphones up
Useless

I realized this was what this trip was going to be like
Every eight or nine seconds
A wretchedly, high-pitched, high-decibel *eeeeek eeeeek!*
On and on
Hundreds of times
A sound that could be used as a sleep deprivation
    torture technique
I swear I was in a machine!

Got me feelin' mean
Feelin bad!
I'm sitting there losing my mind…

"Hey Driver, how do you handle that awful sound?"

"Well, buddy
Some of these bus frames have been renovated top-to-bottom
Twice
Some three times
The Prevost Company out of Dallas does a bang-up job
But, then, so does the road.
Guess y' can just get used t' anything."

"Yeah, driver
Sometimes Greyhound can be a rough ride
But look…
Isn't the Ponchartrain always so spooky at dawn?"

Just twenty-three miles to my city of New Orleans…

"Well, thanks for the ride."

"See ya again some time
Thanks for goin' Greyhound'

Washington, DC 20500

At what junctures during the last few presidencies
Was our pandemic readiness discussed and determined?

250,000 ventilators
Can be stored in a few air-tight warehouses, anywhere
And I'm one of the 370-million citizens
Who did not receive a small box of proper facemasks at my
    front door
At the beginning of this nightmare

May-o-nnaise

Those fighter pilots who fly in from sorties
In thirty-five-million-dollar fighter jets...
They don't 'party'
They don't get high on leave
They keep to rest
And sleep by the clock
Likewise are measured
Breakfast, lunch, and dinner...
At 0400 hours they're on

I once heard from an Airforce photographer
That there was a colonel he knew
Who'd do two lines of high-grade cocaine
Before he flew
Always
When confronted
He told his superiors,
"This is what I do
I wouldn't get in the cockpit without it"
And they let him fly
He was a decorated pilot
Demanding of himself and his team, I imagine
Nothing but the highest standards of performance
And they let it go
Beyond *Top Gun*

And *An Officer and a Gentleman*
(Louis Gossett, Jr. is a beautiful man)

0900 hours…
I'm running late
Is this shirt clean?
Where are my glasses?
And my keys?
Did I take my meds?
Is there gas in the car?
(Yes, there's gas in the car)
Here's my lighter!

We Sat Around

We sat around
While this man dismantled all regulation
Assigning know-nothing puppets
Making a mockery of vital legislation

We sat around
While the water table was contaminated by heavy metals
Lake Pigpen of the Carolinas
Fracking
Fifty states
Each with its own gridlock
Every day

We sat around

Dead Sea Hostel

An old man told us there were leopards in the cliffs

My girlfriend's eyes lit up once she got in the brine,
   waist-deep

The blackrock shale

The Japanese café racers parked in rows

The soldiers with their uzis slung

Must've been a souvenir shop

And a refreshment stand

Up off the road

A grassy knoll

Where I gave my gingey Jill a good rubdown

The small private rooms

With chrome-framed beds

And thin, orange sackcloth-covered mattresses

And the showers and the dining hall

Where that Englishman of what had to be eight decades

Wore those good mountain climbing boots

And thick red socks

He told us about the leopards

I remember his light, almost jovial spirit

And his thin, slightly hunched body

Glad he was to be there on his lonesome

Lit were his blue eyes while he said

"Yes, families of leopards

Up in the red cliffs"

The Magic of Belle Isle
(performed by Morgan Freeman)

"Why don't you write on a computer?"

"Child, I'm going to answer your question
In return for some sweet silence"

"Look at that machine…
A '47 Underwood
I like that you have to write a bit slower on the Manual
I like the way it sounds
I like the way the letters bite into the paper
I like that you can feel it's a genuine human being doing
   the work
That's all…
Now, skedaddle!"

David, Shush!

I was a little kid with a deep voice and thick, curly hair
I landed on competition go-kart tracks
And I opened up gates onto sweltering tennis courts
There was music everywhere
I was popular at school
With two older sisters to dress me up right
I started drinking a tall glass of Café Bustelo
Before school in the fifth or sixth grade
Really...
I'd say I was shy and polite
But with an exclamation point of a personality
And a teddy bear for a girlfriend at fourteen

I guess I peaked kinda early, Doc

No

Paddle boarding:
 No
Kanye:
 No
Go away, man!
Walk California
Bring us something back other than Kanye
Legos into adulthood:
 No
Mars exploratory programs:
 Why?
Let's go to Dubai!
 No
How about Albuquerque?
 God no!
You won't get pregnant if y' do it standing up
 Really?
Fast food past midnight when it's the only thing open:
 No
Dance hall reggae:
 No. What is sacred ground?
Video Games:
 No man — no. Buy a bike; start getting laid
90's anal invasion:
 No ... well.... uh...

More dick jokes from Bill Maher:

  No

An 800-degree planet..........................

Rhino horn powder aphrodisiacs:

  No, man ... That's bad

Tiger bone aphrodisiacs:

  No, man ... That's bad

Street drugs:

  No ... Throw your money in the river

The Amazon rain forest:

  Nature is yucky; New York City is home

Pomegranate juice:

  Almost...

The Köln Concert; Keith Jarret, '75

  You can feel the screws breaking loose

I'm out

Bee-Beeeep (with Dave Bricker)

I've moved into a house on a road in Hollywood, Florida
That's unforgiving and treacherous
These salty, sunny town neighborhoods have a population
   long since overflowed
Into sprawl west of the ocean
West of the Highway
And these roads were kept narrow to maximize lot sizes
Parks, too
But the roads are too narrow to offer any actual safety for
   cyclists in the mix

Taft street is a minor ventricle to Hollywood Boulevard
And Sheridan Street
Both are exits of I-95
And both are main arteries with three lanes of busy traffic
Taft Street provides a secret interior byway
Two lanes of constant activity every workday
Which is what I bring to the forefront here

If and when two cars pass each other going in opposite
   directions
It's tight
With one or two cyclists in the nonexistent bike lanes
There's little room for error
It's a nail-biter

It's treacherous
And you reach it blind

I and many others pack a change of clothing
Wake up earlier
And bike to work
Getting pumped in a good sweat
One towel
One sink
One backpack
One bicycle
One dangerous stretch in Hollywood, Florida

Travel routes for cyclists
Should be diverted into interior neighborhoods

Bike lanes visible
With white reflective lines

Not in twenty years
But now, thank you!

I wonder if a full readout of accidents
Both serious and minor
Might wake somebody the fuck up

There is no median designated 'cause there is no median
The quieter interior streets remain undesignated

The quieter interior streets remain undesignated!

Helmet

Lights

Know where you peddle best, camper!

Two-and-a-Half Again

To be two-and-a-half again
Two-and-a-half again
To see the world anew
And see the world anew again
To pick something up
Just to watch it roll
To climb a little ladder
Slide down a little pole
Two-and-a-half again
Everything's great
And then …

To be two-and-a-half again
Two-and-a-half again
Somebody picks me up
Somebody sets me down
I might talk to myself for half the day
And then not make a sound
Build me a big block house
Without a single worry
I might take my time about it
I might do it in a hurry
Two-and-a-half again
Two-and-a-half again

Oh mama, I'm far enough away
With these little things I do
And these little things I say
But mama…
Not so far
I still need your touch
And to feel your sway

To be two-and-a-half again
Two-and-a-half again
Well that would be a small miracle
Like fitting a square peg into a round hole
Pick me up if I'm crying
Shoulder me out the nearest door
The lights on the boulevard are bright and moving
I'll be asleep by the time we're at the corner
Two-and-a-half again
Two-and-a-half again

I'm waiting for my mom to come
She's on her way home from work
Dad's always got something doin'
I'm two-and-a-half and I hold my own spoon…
If not my own fork
We might shovel sand
Or paint with berries
Mom is soft and sweet

Dad is gruff and hairy
We wrestle on the couch
We swim in the pool
We walk the boardwalk or go to the pier
Pretty soon, we're right outta here

To be two-and-a-half again
Two-and-a-half again
To see the world anew
And then see the world anew again
To pick something up
Just to watch it roll
To climb a little ladder
Slide down a little pole
Two-and-a-half again
Everything's great
And then…

Admission Paper for Rebecca

I am Rebecca Mevlin
I easily consider myself to be
A soul of tested rationality
And balanced consciousness
I am "old school Jewish" in more than ways than one
And it is with something other than intellectual snobbishness
That I greet the world
If history is to be studied from time to time
By artists and poets
The passion of language
Is an apple I've *munched*
Oh, yes…

I am Rebecca Mevlim
Before "Namaste" was a bumper sticker
For the hipper than thou crowd to ridicule
I began practicing the grace of yoga
At twelve years of age
I can lead a crowd of beginners
Or the more advanced Vinyasa practitioners
Anywhere on God's green earth

Coconut Grove was a wonderful place to grow up
My parents were ever vigilant
And naturally affectionate

Three came from them
Ben, myself, and Alex
All of us well-mannered and private school educated
(From an ant farm project it the sixth grade
There still appear unexplained species
Of Africanized insects on our property)

I am Rebecca Mevlinson
My earliest recognition of art
Came in the fourth grade at Palmetto Elementary
I was seated next to Darren Lucas
And Darren could draw!
It was mesmerizing to watch him bring all that Pixar to life
I have since learned
That it was actually Rembrandt
Who invented the television in the 1500s
And Salvador Dali
Who was the first true pornographer
(I let Darren feel me up at a junior high school dance
Don't tell anyone)

To prove what Byron meant to me upon first introduction…
What was Jane Austen's habit of eventually exposing it all?
Who were the "beats?"
What was the million-word club?
How did Hitchens overcome his stuttering?
What planet was Aldous Huxley really from?

I am Rebecca Mevlinowitz
Will I make great art some day?
Maybe a play
That people will choose to swallow
Maybe a book or two
Off in the not-too-very-distant future
That deals with societal issues
No more or less common than my own

I am Rebecca Mevlinstein
Would I like to teach?
Sure…
And at any and all levels for a while
Or maybe write for a periodical of some sort
To cover my bills
That would make me a big girl at twenty-four
I'm aware of the inevitable delivery of invoices

I am Rebecca Mevlinsky…
That's the name they gave me
My earliest of early memories
Is of being read to
Making sure my hands were clean
Before I turned the pages
It was our grandmother
Who we loved most to have read to to us
My *Safta* could not resist

Surrounding us with books
Once she saw that we were collecting
J.K. Rowling's six- and seven-hundred-page editions
I'm sure she took pause
And said to herself
"They're hooked!
We did it!"
Cottage cheese with extra sour cream
Is still this gal's one supreme pleasure
Sitting anywhere
With a cup of something hot

I am Rifka Mevlinovicz
And I'll go read and recite at an open mic any time
So long as there's no TV on
And sufficient light
And some quiet respect
Yes, you go
And for a full hour and forty-five minutes
People vent their manic-depressive chains
And jargoned spirituality
And vespid intellectuality
But then it's your turn
And you recite a poem smart and simple and topical…
And it works!
Like a musician needs a gig to work toward
So should a wordsmith venture out to find

Where he's too sharp
Removed
Depressed
Underground New York…?

I am Rifka Mevlinheimer
And no one calls me Becky
I can change a tire
On an automobile or a ten-speed
Thankyouverymuch
I have had a triple-A card since birth

I am Rebecca Swanson Gayle Mevlína
Community theater can help people
Get to know the power of oratory
So does high school debate club, of course
National Public Radio is a voice in my head
I cannot resist a garage sale
I've heard that crossing Lake Ponchartrain at dawn is
    really something
The Chesapeake Bay Bridge is seventeen-point-six miles long
Niagara Falls probably does something to you down deep
Long-line poetry kicks ass, too, mister
The poetry of the impoverished
Is the voice of having just that much to hold on to
They win

I am Rebecca Mevlin

And I had some help writing this tardy admission application

He's a poet named Lev…

Maiche Lev

He stays in our guest house once in a while

Here by Kennedy Park

He hardly knows me at all

He ran up a cable bill you would not believe!

He fed me the idea for the format:

"My name is…"

He told me I'd better send it

As those admission committees get bored as hell

So *en finale*

To be in New York City

Free to read and study and write

And love New York City…

Upon delivering me to Brandeis University a few years back

My father

Mr. Joshua Mevlin

Grasped my shoulders firmly

Before leaving me in Waltham

He said, "Child…

For how many born on this earth…

How many get the chance to stand where you stand now?"

And he said it to me again

Losing it a little

"How many born on this globe get to stand where you
    stand now?"
He put his palms to my cheeks
And pulled my head to his heart

And somebody down the hall lit a joint
And…

Two-room Apartments

If you had these quarters on a cruise ship
You'd be riding high on the *Queen Mary*
You're doin' alright…
Make the most of it!

Call us if you need anything…
Bye!

Tiger Tiger

Futon

Feng shui

Shiatzu

Namaste…?

Tai-chi

Karaoke

Sushi-yama

Nagasaki

Godzilla

Fuji-mori

Fushu-Daiko

Hari-kari

Jiu-jitsu

Hot saki

Now I want to play with your feet!

Kimono

Mitsubishi

Buddokan

Kei Pè

Yoko Ono

Konichiwa

Daniel-san!

Honda

Acura

Kawasaki

Hollywood!
Hollywood!
Take a piss!
Take a piss!

My Staple

Two cups of coffee

Three bananas (very yellow)

Peanut butter powder (2 *heaping* tablespoons)

Almond milk (2 cups)

Granola (½-cup)

A dash of ginger

Top off with ice

And two shakes of ground cinnamon

Blend till smooth

Enjoy!

Globetrotters

I saw Curly Neal
And Meadowlark Lemon
On the same court

I must've done somethin' right
Somewhere
Sometime
On the Astral plane

.

Concerts of My Youth

Stevie Wonder

I saw Stevie Wonder at the Sunrise Musical Theater. His backing band was *his* backing band, "Wonderbug." They were all masters of funk ... *masters*.

And just like his music on the radio made our listening landscape so golden, at the theater, with its 4,700 seats full, Stevie Wonder ruled all night just off center-stage on his keyboard throne. Love, tears, gold ... woven together tight.

And me ... all of fourteen or fifteen ... not smart enough yet to bogart somebody's joint.

The Stones

I saw The Stones a few times at big venues. Once, I went alone with Upper Deck Orange Bowl "fear of heights" bleacher seats. I couldn't boogie really, but then I honed in on Ronnie Wood and Keith, and this time I took that joint.

Charlie Watts... It was falling axes, mud and mudslides, slide guitar whiplash. And then they went into "Ain't No Use in Cryin'" or "Tops" or ...

Not any of 'em gonna ever give up their rock 'n' roll shoes.

Bruce Springsteen

Your first Springsteen show stays with ya. We were *losin'* it at the Hollywood Sportatorium with the **E Street Band.**

We went with my math tutor, David Altshuler, who'd spent the previous three summers traveling, scalping tickets, seeing shows, and selling bootlegged concert shirts. On the way to the show, he asked us what songs we wanted to hear most. I don't remember what the other fellas asked for, but I said I wanted to hear "Thunder Road" twice. We all laughed. David drove a twenty-year-old Chevy Impala that had been handed down as a hand-me-down … and at the Sportatorium parking lot, he managed to upgrade our tickets.

We were all 13 years old. I connected with the songs; we all knew 'em—Joel and Jimmy and Sean and Stoneberg… the idea of Bruce was just so exciting.

The show came to its end after the "Detroit Medley" with "Street Fighting Man."

So much driving high energy from this band! 17,500 people had just been through something. We felt like we could fly!

To get up closer, I crawled under the seats to get to the front rows. Bruce Springsteen was on a rear top riser going into the Stones tune I didn't exactly know. The raucous first strum had us.

I'd been moving between people's feet and hotdog wrappers. I surfaced into a Fender Telecaster, right there! "Everywhere I hear the sound of marching, charging feet, boy!"

After the show, as though affected by something just barely legal—or lethal, we piled in that moldy Impala and went to Denny's. I ordered *two* milkshakes—vanilla—for my hoarse voice. For days after, we walked around not knowing what we were going to do with our lives.

Your first Springsteen show stays with you.

Neil Young

That man! At the James L. Knight Center, sometime toward the end of the first set, a bunch of people wanted to be closer to him and they rushed the stage. Neil Young looked at them and said, "You're too good to me."

In Neil's early work, there's a mystical poet who can't be reached. To know it, you have to study it in some other vein. On Rock 'n' Roll's Rushmore, that's him lookin' out—so spooky. That man.

Carlos Santana

The *I'm Winning* Tour came to Sunrise and I sat stage-left-center, first fifteen rows. His longtime percussionists included the drummer he used at Woodstock, Michael Shrieve. Another was a dark-haired Latino who Carlos must have probably met on the streets of LA somewhere—*killin'* it!

When they did "Black Magic Woman," the guy next to me shot up out of his seat. Someone gave me a few pulls off a hash pipe … and what a dance I did. They should name a spice after Santana.

Prince once said he most admired Santana's guitar playing, saying, "He could lift people out of their seats with one note."

Bob Dylan

I went to the show with Todd Micheals, a senior at Beach High. I was a ninth grader. I think my best friend, Scott Davis was

with us, and another older friend of Todd. We sat stage left ...
no ... stage right.

Dylan was touring his *Shot of Love* '81 release. I didn't know
how much I would love and rely on that record until much later.

Dylan's light show was memorable insomuch that he at-
tempted to cast a fluorescent, black-and-white effect on the
stage — like being in a business office at 2:00 with nothing going
on. He wore Jimmy Page-like flared black pants and a dragon
kimono. He wore dark sunglasses the whole show. At the end
of the final encore, he took 'em off for a so-long gesture and
Todd said, "There he is!"

Dylan with double drums. Jim Keltner and the cat who
played on "Blood on the Tracks." His girls singing in
burgundy church flowing robes. Mavis Staples, Clydie King,
Madeleine Quebec: the queens of rhythm. From *Slow Train
Coming* through *Saved* and *Shot of Love,* they've toured and
recorded with him. After the show, my friend Sean Edelson
and his father waited at the loading bay and got to meet
the girls.

Jim Keltner had three mounted tom-toms plus three more.
He went for a trash can effect.I remember how he wrapped
around the set while the other drummer filled in, skiffling
a lot.

Sometime during the show, Todd's friend offered me and my
buddy, Scott, a toke. We both said, "No ... No, thanks, man!"
We must've been 14 years old. That's when it all started.

James Taylor

He seemed to come to Sunrise every other year. My sister brought roses and gave 'em to him when he came out. He bent down and took them, thanking her. In the spotlight, she kissed his cheek. My Jan-Jan … with short hair and electric-blue eyes. I'll never forget.

Dan Dugmore was the drummer. He wore a tank-top and kept a white towel within reach. He *satisfied*. *All business.* Understated until thunderous.

Leland Sklar on bass. He went out with Phil Collins next. Imagine what it takes to play *Sussudio,* even once.

But Sweet Baby James, he's always been too beautiful for this world. He's a master. You're in the same room with that voice, the songs, the vintage instruments they've chosen coming through the state-of-the-art sound system.

The greats: They come to town, they set up, they play, and they're down the road. J.T.'s one of 'em and we're the better for it. That American son lookin' on like only the Carolina woods could tap.

The Kinks

My first rock show. Sunrise. Row double-X. Dead center.

And who's sitting right next to me but Lisa Zaiac, the girl I was bar-mitzvah with not a year before.

The music was slamming loud like that aspirin commercial on TV in the 70s.

Ray Davies was handsome and thin with his mischievous, gap-tooth smile. Brother Dave wore his black Gibson Les Paul like it weighed more than him. And his maroon number, the same. Irresistible English classic electric crunch.

The crowd bayed to "Lola" from the first strum. And then the sweetness of "Shangri-La" and "Celluloid Heroes."

The Kinks live beyond their name.

Row XX.

13 years old

One for the Road — Live

Willie Nelson

Hey Willie!

I've seen Willie Nelson four or five times through the years. Everybody has a few favorite Willie songs. "Blue Eyes Cryin' in the Rain," "Angel Flyin' Too Close to the Ground," "Seven Spanish Angels..."

At one concert, down near Key West, the Willie Nelson Family were so *on.* Jill wrote down all the numbers Willie played, and she declared post-concert that they'd done 43 songs!

Willie and sister Bobbie and the whole family were a class act. None of that bullshit swagger that's so sickening in a lot of Country-Western music — none of that dumb, drunk, patriotic hoo-hah. Willie walks the line without skirting the flag.

The Marley Family

Ziggy was holy in white linens, long, enviable dread at the Bicentennial Park Amphitheater. I was up close, stage-right.

There was a lightning storm. I danced reggae so much I had a hint of blood in my urine the next day.

During the show, the band settled into a long breakdown and all the little Marleys came ambling out like little ska babies, the cutest thing my eyes have ever witnessed. Six-to-ten little dreadlocked munchkins. *On it!*

Shalom Salaam. Salaam Shalom.

Sheryl Crow

Chicago. I was on a road trip with a nutty Jewish gal, supporting the Miami Beach Senior High School Rock Ensemble being honored at the Rock-n-Roll Hall of Fame in Cleveland. The band, with director Doug Burris, played a gig in Illinois at the Hard Rock Café before going on to Ohio.

So, me and Miss Nutty Buddy — with a belly-full of psilocybin mushrooms — we go up into the Sears Tower and do a Ferris Bueller, melting fuzzily as we were. And on the way down, we see an announcement on the little electronic ticker tape that Sheryl Crow is playing that night in the city somewhere.

Tickets! Sheryl! Baby!

For the encore she revealed that she likes to wear ruffled, old fashioned, long, ladies' underwear by mooning the crowd from her piano seat.

They played the song "Safe and Sound," which is the greatest fucking piece of music ever made.

By the time we got back to our so-so hotel, the wind and weather caused me to realize I needed to actually thaw — *fucking thaw* — me and my girlfriend and my dog.

Yes, we traveled 3,000 miles with my black labrador, Boozoo. I think the three of us could have been caught howling 'cause thawing is achy-breaky … and we are Florida sun babies. That town's a little too rough for me.

Sheryl Crow: So much talent! She rocked that opera house!

Hole

Anyhow, by the time we got back south into Florida, we learned that Courtney Love and her band "Hole" were playing in Fort Lauderdale.

Some guy in the lobby asked me if I was "alright."

Me? Yeah. Why?

The songs were amateur — unmemorable — but Courtney is forever babe-a-licious. The house was all-girl … and all mad.

She was in that Larry Flynt movie. And, Sid and Nancy, No?

I wonder what a tragic malcontent like her dreams of. And I wonder what her relationship with her daughter, Bean, is like.

The Grateful Dead

I seen 'em maybe a dozen times. I only once had a kind of hallucination — Dali-esque — in a Miami show. His elephants' pogo-sticks-for-legs came steppin' across the stage like a holographic parade.

When they played "Fennario," I could have burst, harmonizing exaltedly with arms raised. I remember the kids outside the Atlanta Omni rattling the modern art. I remember this skateboarder at Stone Mountain, *giving* himself to the downhill curve.

I swam in a cold river one year. I had on a shorty wetsuit and it was *cold* water, like maybe in the low 60s. And just downriver my light — my heart — started a-blinkin'. When I finally reached the shore my legs wouldn't work. Jill was alarmed. "Somebody build a fire!" My buddy Noah Klein said, "Breathe."

That night Mickey Hart on the drum riser used a jackhammer on some kind of metal slab. A microphone on that kind 've *shatter* … with fifteen-thousand people tripping…!

People handing out nitrous balloons in CRUSH RUSH tee-shirts.

People offering up potato-leek soup.

Skeleton tie-dye everywhere.

Made me … subconsciously … balked!

And all y' hear in the lot is the sound of other shows, from tours recent and past.

The Dead. What a scene!

Those tricksters in the sound booth are doing a little more than just balancing the band's sound, man. They have a hand-ful of tricks f' ya head.

That jackhammer…!

Christ!

Steve Van Zandt

Anytime you get a chance to talk about his '82 release, *Men Without Women,* y' take it.

There were twenty people on Miami Beach who knew that record existed ... and my eight closest friends were the half. We were fifteen and this album was like owning the world!

I saw Southside Johnny and the Asbury Jukes in Jacksonville. They played half of *Men Without Women*. I didn't know if I should sit there and love it, or if I should reach up and touch the sky. Did some of both.

When I saw Steve Van Zandt in Fort Lauderdale a couple of weeks after Tom Petty died, he opened up with "Even the Losers."

Jimmy Buffet

Gusman Hall, '83. Gusman Hall is a 1500-seat opera house in the heart of Miami—a fixture still, a city's prize.

Jimmy Buffet wore white leather and played his white, hollow-body Gibson guitar. The Coral Reefers sextet was a virtuosic punch. Just brilliant! The whole band workin' and nobody steppin' on anyone's feet.

I had the album *Volcano* on 8-track tape from years before. "Les Petits Enfants" is one of God's favorites. And there really is a Mr. Utley ... and a Mango Man...

And Jimmy Buffet ... I think I went the second night, too. I recorded the concerts on a Sony Walkman, and I met my friend, Doris Maya, by the soundboard. "Hey, Dori!"

Jackson Browne

He got to the Sunrise stage late as he'd been at a protest for something elsewhere in the northeast. He announced to the crowd upon taking the stage, "Sorry I'm late…. I'm a fucking asshole."

Mountain flutes through microphones. Jackson Browne is forever the coffee and the cream.

The Psychedelic Furs

Gusman Hall. Richard Butler's voice 'll send a chill up your spine. (Punk was a strange patch of my adolescence).

An upperclassman was acting out his punk fantasy and so we followed along for a few weekends. We'd pile into his big Buick and drink beer and go out and break stuff for fun. I mean we'd ace a parked Datsun like little hellions. And The Clash was the soundtrack. I haven't thought of that in eons!

Bobby McFerrin

At a Danky War Memorial in West Miami. I had front row seats. A man and a microphone. I gave myself to his every run. I think I distracted him from the audience. They weren't all busy giving themselves to his rhythmic and vocal cornucopia.

Tom Petty

At RFK Stadium, before a song, he proclaimed, "It was never this orange before."

In Miami, he said, "We're gonna be up here until we feel like we've really played."

In Gainesville: "In case you're not sure if you got the right tickets, I am Tom Petty and these are the Heartbreakers. Look around; we've got the makings of a big-time rock-and-roll show here."

His guitarist and best friend, Mike Campbell arousing roses from the big speakers'—stems and all. I love to see him work.

Nick Lowe warmed up for Tom at the Palm Beach Amphitheater back when I was in high school.

I do believe I had *Damn the Torpedoes* on 8-track, too.

Lenny Kravitz opened for Tom in Miami. Lenny's dreadlocks and his dance, and his power-paw guitar.

My wife thought he was *something* … and he must've been—he's openin' up for T.P.

Hey Lenny…

The Police

Hollywood Sportatorium, '82. "Ghost in the Machine" tour. Front-row seats. My friend Michael Sherota's folks got us the tickets. I watched Stewart Copeland fly on his TAMAs all night.

Andy Summers—with his Schecter/Fender guitars—he played so atmospherically and odd. *Genius!* All in the key of the undiscovered chord.

And then … Sting!

A yellow-feathered bass Duvalier!

Me and 17,000 people getting' it from a trio—a trio! The Police were no trick or gimmick. Driving artists. So young.

They're so elegant … and it's reggae!

Oh!

Thanks, Mike!

Billy Joel

"Allentown" tour and the one after that, both at the Hollywood Sportatorium.

Multi-instrumentalist sax dude with a sledgehammer and an anvil. A factory whistle—really blew! Liberty DeVitto on TAMA kit. Billy Joel's voice so signature.

I got punished for sneaking out of the house to go his second show on his second night.

"But it was Billy Joel!"

"You're punished."

"But it was Billy Joel, the piano man!"

"You're still punished."

The only stage background was black ruffled fabric and some ramps.

Yes

Trevor Rabin just *had* to play a standout electric guitar solo…

Because Steve Howe…

Steve Howe's J-45!

Butter!

Jon Anderson was all there. He wore a short cape (Not everyone can do that).

People say Yes is "too much." But thank God for them.

Béla Fleck and the Flecktones

Con Edison in New York to Florida Power and Light.

'Nuff said.

Hardpack (with D. Bricker)

The beach in Jacksonville is hardpack
Due to fine sediment accumulating there for millennia
Almost as solid as asphalt
The Gulfstream
An endless river
The eastern shore of the peninsular state
Its sieve
When dry
The soft winds gather silt
Bites like a sandstorm at your knees, chest, and face
Clear your throat with a cold beer
I could live there forever

Apart from the people with houses on the Atlantic
There's no big money anywhere
When work is over at 5:00
The people get on their bikes with the wind in their hair
And ride around with the surfers and children and dogs
Every handlebar with a custom-made drink-holder
The sands turn orange
Five miles south of Punta Gorda
Before Verano Beach
A few beers
A few joints
And whatever else…

America happens there
Surf's up!
An old yellow Corvette
A big community Church
Crabbing 'neath the bridges
A favorite diner

I've written about Jax before
But that beach…!
The Navy Warships
The St. John's River
The mosntrous step-up transformers over the glades
The little place that serves only soup
And that band that played the Irish Samuel Adams ballad
And the other band of old hippies
Laying down Fleetwood Mac just like the record…
And the surf shops?
My God!
Kids on skateboards like dragonflies

I'm gonna go back there
And stay a year…
Or until I've had enough
Take a little Tennessee bikini for my own
Set her up and disappear
Draw a mosaic — a busy mural — on the hardpack everyday

Where's Joe?

The funniest political joke I've heard this year is:

"You gotta keep an eye on Joe

Or he might just wander away"

Simone

The angry black woman on SNL is unidimensional
  and annoying
I wish she'd lose forty pounds and suddenly be someone else
Lorne would have to expand her portfolio
And the still-viewing public would come to admire an
  African-American female
Who could take herself by the hand and redefine herself
I bet she already has…
I haven't watched Saturday Night Live in a long, long time
Other than to catch my boy, Seth nightly
And that Jimmy Fallon's doin' alright for himself these
  days, too
Isn't he?

Oh God! No Sugar Babies

Where's my SweeTarts?

My Nutty Buddy?

My Charleston Chew?

Pixie Stix?

Atomic Fireballs?

Jawbreakers?

Chunky?

Snickers?

Milky Way?

Goobers?

Raisinettes?

Zagnut?

Butterfinger?

Clark bar?

Razzles?

Skittles?

Zazzles?

Zotz?

Whoppers?

Jujubes?

Milk Duds?

Bit-o-Honey?

Ladyfingers?

Lemonheads?

Good 'n' Plenty?

Mounds!

M & Ms!
Reese's!
Now & Later!
Chiclets
Hot Tamales!
Twinkies!

The weird thing is y' never see anybody buyin' this stuff
Even kids…

Wonderbread…!
Deep-fried sticks of butter

The soaring price of insulin
One-in-three are borderline diabetic
Big sugar
Thievery!
Big sugar
Bloody murder!

Biker Gangs

Biker gangs…
The patch
Wanna come over and make forts?
I dare ya to jump
There's no one's mother around to say, "It's time to go home"
You won't be happy until someone gets hurt
I said, "You won't be happy until someone gets hurt"

Biker gangs
They don't like your orange van
They don't like your sandals
They…
They do like your girlfriend
Do not underestimate them
They are to be avoided
Before they kill each other off
They'll do harm a-plenty
Scary dudes
Bad hombres
Who like to inspire fear
Who likes to inspire fear?

Be someone
Teach a kid to throw

Biker gangs

Embarrassing, isn't it…?

More has been said than this

Its 2:00
Stay Tuned for Folk and Acoustic Music
(with Dave Bricker)

I know Michael Stock
But he wouldn't know me
I knew him back at "Our Place"
With little Amani cutting carrots in the kitchen
He hosted the open mic
That was some gray hairs ago

When my son Levi played little league
At Flamingo Park on Miami Beach
Michael was there with his daughter and his wife
Those were nice afternoons
In the shadows of the racquetball courts
That banyan tree soaked up with sun out in deep left
His kid broke her arm one year

And then…
"Hey, Michael Stock,"
At the guitar show
In the Convention Center
By the escalators
I was with my American Indian friend, Tyrone Ludwig
A great player in his own right

The show was an expensive flop
But a cool display of guitars
For the people who love them

I saw the man at the art district in Wynwood
And the day after Thanksgiving in Greynolds Park
There was Michael
Joshing around the "Lumpy Sue Festival"
People streaking into the lake
Man... that water's kinda cold!

Michael is a particular kind of Jewish person
Ashkenazic
He's got a vibe
Kinda like there's a light bulb that goes on in his head when-
    ever he smiles
That effusive smile he can't repress
Absolutely
If he was a "hugger" we'd all be in trouble
I had a friend who didn't like him for this happy trait
It almost seems pretentious but it isn't
The light goes on and he can't help it...
Or he can't help it and the light goes on...
Either way
When you see him with his wife
She's the more serious type
So he doesn't just fly away, I suppose
Their kid's probably well out of college by now

I don't know if they had any other little "Stocks" but
   all the best

Michael was upstate
At the Gamble Rogers State Park dedication a few years back
East coast of Florida
Groovy place
Groovy storyteller and fingerpicker
The much-loved Gamble Rogers

I played on his radio show in the NPR studios in '85
After I played the intro at Live Aid
I was at a friend's house in Miami Beach
The Stonebergs
And my friend Dave's father came in
And told me the DJ was calling me on the air
To come on down…
So I did
In my old green Starfire GT
I made it across Biscayne Bay and they let me in
I had my guitar and, say, two songs other than
"Knocking on Heaven's door"
And "Tangled Up in Blue"
And he interviewed me
About the song I'd played in Philly weeks before
"You're Bernard Watson?"
"Yeah"
(I don't know a single verse of that song, today)

Michael Stock *loves* Michael Hedges
Still plays him often
Hedges died suddenly years ago
But he was the best acoustic guitar player anywhere
On earth…
Ever
He'd paid some dues and wasn't a prick
His death really surprised and saddened Stock
Probably saddened a lot of others too

On Michael's show
Y'always gotta kinda legitimize yourself
With the standard Stockian question:
"What do you do? Are you a full-time musician?"
"Well, no
I rob banks, Michael…"

Stock is a regular at the Luna Star Café
And at two, maybe three-hundred house concerts
I think he and local gem Diane Ward
Might have somethin' goin' on
If you're smoking a joint
He'll take a hit or two
(I've seen it)
On the radio he doesn't enunciate "NPR" quite well enough
But don't tell anyone

I'll go to his funeral if he beats me there
I'll play harmonica after the burial
In the parking lot with my yamaka on my head
And some white face make-up
Like Bob Dylan wore on the "Rolling Thunder Review"
Promise!
(I want my funeral to be at a petting zoo
You can spread my ashes all over the llama)

Stay tuned for more folk and acoustic music
Oh, I sat near him at the Dan Burn Show
In Coconut Grove's Space Transit Planetarium
During the show
Between songs
Dan asked, "What's the name of this place?"

I'm glad to put this song together
This letter
This writing
These words
Mike's a good guy
And he deserves something like this in a book
I knew it'd be fun as soon as I plucked the idea
Michael Stock
Sure I know him
But he wouldn't know me

I bet he never goes anywhere
Without someone calling out his name
Hey ... Michael Stock!
Must drive his wife crazy!

— October, 2019

Stevia

If you microwave your coffee
And it has "Equal" or "Sweet-n-Low" in it
You could get Alzheimer's disease
Or maybe Parkinson's, too

Try Stevia!

Sweets

And Kellogg's and Keebler and Pepperidge Farms
And Hostess and Nabisco
How does it feel to be somebody's diabetic cash cow?
Someone's trained pallet?
A Dairy Queen demographic?

I'm only seeing this for the first time, too

My confectionary guilty pleasure?
I've always loved MaryJanes
And anything caramel
Who can resist walnut Toblerone?
My first wife used to fill her palm with M&Ms…
And *wuff*'em!
(She'll kill me)

I can remember my silver fillings
Disintegrating into a Now & Later back in my youth
God!
A single Sugar Daddy could do *hundreds of dollars* in damage

On an acid trip in Amsterdam
This dude I was hanging with
Sent us on a wild goose chase through the city
To find Chips Ahoy and milk

My dad could market his caramel popcorn
Neighbors call, asking for it
And then ... rugela ... baklava ... halvah

Smokey marshmallows around the campfire
Beneath the moon
It's therapy...

And a Hershey's Kiss for your bellybutton, baby...

Thanks to Bill and Steve

People complain that all these new gadgets are
    attention thieves

Before the modern pocket computer
Only a small population of women kept address books

Consider the expanse of universal neural activity…
People used to just sit at bus stops
Staring off

Gator in the Front Yard

The gator and the boa eye-to-eye weren't friends

The boa did as a boa does

And wrapped around the gator's knobby gator skin

The redneck in the airboat took a picture with a grin

The gator twisted

The boa's grip slipped

And then…

That gator knew this invasive species tasted *just like chicken*

Sorry, Ed

I just had to put a dog to sleep
He was a rescued animal who followed his growl
I took good care of him for nearly two-and-a-half years
He was two
A full grown adolescent when he and I first went on the prowl

His brain had wasted in the *cruel* tropical South Florida sun
No water
Always tied
People who let suffering be brought to God's creatures
Should have the same shown their hide

His name was Ed
That's what Griselda from the agency told us
Ed
She pulled up in a black tank
He had *both* fleas and ticks
"If you have any trouble, call us"

He was a dog who followed his growl
He would sing when I played the harp
Made me laugh every time
A beautiful howl

He was pretty
A pretty, smallish black lab mix at 62 pounds

For two years we walked together
In the "house help" part of town

He slept at the foot of my bed
He definitely had some pit bull in him
Y' could tell by his jaw and widened head
Ed was a junkyard dog
Best kept close when out walkin'
And I stand in question of my decision
To put him down
Ed was Ed
My Ed

He was sweet
And I quickly learned to love him
And he loved me as his active master
He deserved to live as much as anything alive
Which brings us back to rescue
And disaster

For days I agonized over what had to be done
For days I looked away from him
I tilted my head back
And shed a tear in the kitchen

I had to …
Because he was not to be trusted

A young kid at the back porch of my house
It was his impulse to follow his growl
The sliding glass door nearly busted
Teeth drawn in his mouth

The lady who brought me the dog, Griselda
It was her very own animal rescue operation
Here's a loaded gun …
No it's not the kind of gun that sits in a box at the top of
   the closet
It doesn't have a safety
Four legs and a tail
Tightly wound
Click
Flesh and bone in a single round

To me he was a companion
Who was just better kept close
At the beach at night
He'd lunge
At anyone who approached
At the dog park
He was the dominant alpha host

Every animal on God's green earth
Deserves its chance to live
Sure as they're born

Sure as they're born
Yesterday I counted 23 kids in the village
As I contemplated this dog's day in the corn

Damaged goods
Good intentions versus reality
You can't exactly shank this off on another adoption agency
They don't learn what you know …
Until it's too late
Here comes Ed scramblin' down another hallway
Same story with a new name
"Liability"
My liability

Like the snapping of that possum's neck
Ed was real direct
Oh, it is a noble thing
To save the injured and neglected
The condemned
This dog followed his growl
Ready to kill
To maim
Something was deeply wrong within him

A killing machine
Oh, they're home from school
A kid with a Frisbee at the back door …

A vicious sound
Mean and cruel

I had to have him put down
He was an angel someone made into a demon
I gave him all a pet owner can give
My place is empty now
No sad eyes, big and brown
He didn't deserve to die
But, where in this world could he live?

That dog
So loveable to me
So pretty, wild, and free at the beach
There was no place for him to go
I called around
I ended up calling a trainer or two
Talked to each

I searched
To see if there might be some place like a ranch
Where a dog can run free
He told me straight out that no such place exists
That place is a myth
I thanked him for having listened to me
And I called the Humane Society

I am not a terribly indecent person
You adopt a dog
You're in for a ride
Sometimes you've just got to accept
Those things your heart would keep denied

I told this trainer fella exactly what I've told you here
I told him that I absolutely reject the idea
That this could be trained out of him
This much to me about Ed was clear

God forbid!
Y' don't get another chance
When a child's neck is snapped
The coffee table's corners
Running with scissors
Stairways
Outlets
Fingers
Your baby's in the bushes
Door's not quite shut
A mission for mourners

Awful, all around
What to do?
Can't just let it be
It's not about fitting in here

It's about being up-front
It's about bottom-line responsibility

Ed
Wild Ed
He bit my roommate
He bit him on the hand
All my roommate did was look for his shoe
Underneath the bed stand
That's where my girlfriend's child plays

He bit the U-Haul lady
He bit someone in the alley
He scared half the neighborhood
Scared Shelley, my secretary

I adopted a dog
Dog had a vicious streak
I didn't know it until I let him off his leash
Late at night he'd go after that possum
Alley cats
Skateboarders
You name 'em

I walked out of the humane society in Jacksonville thinking
I sure hope there's room for him somewhere
Pepper and Rocky and Mozel and Boozoo

And Ed …
So sorry, Ed …
There was little else I could do
It wasn't because I didn't care

"Pothe"

My parents could never have known
That my real name
Was Apothecary Bromeliade
My friends just call me "Pothe"

It's Robert Fripp and his League of Crafty Guitarists
It's the Penguin Café Orchestra
It's "Oh my gosh…
I haven't owned a pair of Birkenstocks in years!"
It's the woman you marry
And stay with for fifty years

Pothe?
Yes … with an e at the end…
A silent e
Pothe is a cutie who draws well…
Pothe is one who daydreams effectively
Pothe is kind…
Once he found himself without one of his very own kind

Pothe is…
The second set in Hampton which was "Bob-heavy"
"China Rider"
"Scarlet"
"Fire"

"Help"
"Slip Franklin into Jimmy"
"Drum Space"

Hey, Pothe!

Hey, Man
Don't stay with those squirt bottles, dude
Pothe, have a good show
Pothe?

Ha Ha Ha

People do like to laugh
Like a child likes to be played with
Or chased
Put on or tickled
It's the most natural thing in the world
Laughter
People *love* to laugh
Funny is funny
Slapstick
Clever
Irony
The satirical

The funniest thing happened to me today, honey
I've got a funny story to tell you
Funny thing about it was…
That's funny, man
Muddy Waters said, "I have *lots* of fun"

I let out a little laugh the other day
And realized it had been some time since
A syllable of laughter had crossed my lips
A chuckle

In high school I guess I had more than a few laughs
But it was no joke when college acceptance letters came

And I wasn't goin' anywhere but nowhere
Go Dawgs!

Do all fathers let out an occasional howl
While watching TV in bed with mom?

I laughed so hard I peed in my pants
He had 'em rollin' in the isles
Carlin
Pryor
Foxworthy
And the incomparable Texan, Ron White
Does your dog bite?

Wanna hear a funny joke?
No, but go ahead…
Whaddya call a poet who's got nothin' to say?
Funny, funny
Ha, ha
Everybody's smilin' but me

False laughter is almost demonic
And laugh machines may signal the apocalypse
Happiness comes suddenly
And leaves just as quick

She was the kind of person who said things that weren't all
    that funny

But I loved her funny face
And I knew as soon as we met
That even when we were old
I would have a kiss for her

Well, uh … that's a funny way of lookin' at things
Ace Ventura: Pet Detective was a classic
Beyond slapstick funny
But the sequel he did for thirty-million dollars was an insult
Comedy isn't pretty

I fail to find *any* of this amusing
I'm here with my date
And this amateur at the open mic
Has nothing to offer but profanity
What…? Are you mad at your mother?

If you've got ten dollars
Y' can make yourself merry
If y' only got a dime
It's the Staten Island ferry[2]

The world's unfunniest videos
Congratulations…
First Prize … one week in Philadalphia
Second prize…

---

2   Bob Dylan, "Hard Times in New York Town"

I got fun
You want some?
God!

Ain't it like ... something's funny
'Bout spending someone else's money[3]

She doesn't think he's very funny anymore
No... She used to laugh when we were dating

Just think about the fool
Who by his virtue can be found
In a most unusual situation
Playin' jester to the clowns[4]

If you're happy and you know it...

---

3   Jacob Dylan, "Somebody Else's Money"
4   Lightfoot, Gordon. "Race Among the Ruins"

Two Guys; Same Girl

Jeff: Hey Andrew, y' see that blonde across the street?

Andrew: Yes, stout and cheeky is she

Jeff: She's got great ██!

Andrew: Well, bold she is, Jeff

Jeff: Man, Andrew, she's got *back. You don't see white girls with that boss an* ██!

Andrew: Andrew, my friend, she is a woman of rare form

Jeff: I wanna ██ her, man. *Ewwee! I could* ██ her till we was both sweatin' hard

Andrew: To lay with her could lead to games of the most sweetly sinful kind, you might say

Jeff: I wonder what kind of ████ she has...

Andrew: Woman is a delightful creature

Jeff: I can see myself playing '██ ██ ██' with her

Andrew: Oh, again Andrew, you touch upon the effervescence of physical ecstasy and love

Jeff: Andrew, she's a real blonde... Think she's ██?

Andrew: A blessing it is upon mankind that we are polymorphously perverse

Jeff: I want her! That██! Dirty blond ██ ██! Ooh ... Can't get her out of my mind!

Andrew: Your brief obsession will pass, Andrew

Jeff: No, man; I'm gonna have to ██ ██ in the shower!

Andrew: Continued news of your lustful drive is of little concern to me, Andrew

Jeff: Andrew, What are you always thinkin' of 'n' ██? ██ I feel like I need an excuse...

Andrew: An *excuse?*

Jeff: Yeah, an excuse, Andrew ... to speak ... to be as good as you, man

Andrew: Oh ... I'll take a handful of ██ and a mouthful of ██ any time

Jeff: (Laughter)

Greyhound on Canal

In the New Orleans Greyhound station
The homeless got things timed
In the New Orleans Greyhound station
Watch your things
There's an art to petty crime
In the New Orleans Greyhound station
The baggage handlers smoke
I been halfway 'round this country on these buses
And nowhere else have I seen 'em … smokin'

Somethin' about the skies above the city
The great swamp down below
Your Mighty Mississippi
Royal Street in the mid to late afternoon
There'll be another 24-hour joint
Opening up around here soon
There's always a bunch of *bad* cats
Congregating around Lee Circle
Last week they flew General Robert E. Lee out by helicopter
Now they got Professor Longhair up there
Smilin' away with his full gold dental (Yeah!)

In New Orleans they got trolleys
On St. Charles, you ride pass Rite-Aid
And suddenly everything gets green and beautiful
Like it's a new little town you've never been to

The whole place is still mom 'n' pop alley
Yes it is, by Golly!
Really…
Burger King and McDonald's haven't opened up anyplace
Musta been the music's too loud!
'No such thing as a Po Boy Whopper!
'No such thing as any McCrawfish McMuffin
Nope!

N'awlins
N'awlins
N'awlins
Had the same bricks since 1726

This N'awlins
Improvements?
We don't do *improvements*

This the Big Easy
Ya gotta make it last!
Low budget. Everybody's sweatin' rent

Shorty, there's a beeline parade today
Comin' up offa Rampart
I think that's what I heard
Shorty, you heard about it?

Last summer I was there
I didn't greet the dawn once
Now *that* is a crime
Fog rolls through less in June…
But morning's in November
It's like there's ghosts…
A cup of coffee in New Orleans still only costs a dime

N'awlins is great
But don't go wanderin' away
Night or day
Your girlfriend there
Keep her close
In your pocket
There's *no* opportunity
No one has a job

Hey, Shorty
You got a clean shirt I could borrow?"
Labor Pool down on Tchoupitoulas
Think it was yes'day they say come t'morrah, Shorty

New Orleans Sheraton Hotel
1:00 Sunday afternoon

"You got everything, honey?"
"Yep, I'll go downstairs and check out

Got the pralines for John
The Dilly Beans for Debra
Chicory for your sister
That tee-shirt Tim asked for
And enough beignet mix for six months of Sundays, baby!"

The New Orleans 9:20
Now boarding!
SlidellGulfportBiloxiMobilePensacolaFortWaltonPanamaCityTallahassee!
And all points east

To Pope Branuff and his Jet Ski Cronies

All kidding aside
Right now I live in a house in a mixed neighborhood
A man was shot to death robbing a convenience store
A while before I got here
My neighbor, Roy, borrowed some small bills
Got high
Beat his girl one night
They came crashing through my front door
In full Springer, fighting on
The cops came
He's been in jail for six weeks
Now his son doesn't have money for anything

The poor are depressed in the blight of it all
Getting high is the only real escape
A temporary out…
But an *out*
Life becomes cheap and tears flow and mothers wail
And rap is always a little harder to hear

I'm white and so are my sisters
And if one of them had brought home a black man
No matter how well adjusted he was
It'd take my Dad some getting used to
But, I know that if the Negro race had been introduced to
    our bloodline

Their beautiful soft traits
Their strongest dread
Their princely form and boldness
Would have been ten-thousand blessings for us

The global oligarchy builds in space now
Children fall behind never to catch up
Never
School is ten months of *what?*
Whatever priorities of the ultra-wealthy that got them so rich
The problems they could solve today…
Build up these ghettos
Refurbish and stock these schools
Make it happen in one generation
Make it rain
Here and now
What word be left of you!
All kidding aside

Munich

In the spirit of the Olympiad
The 1972 Munich games
Are officially cancelled
Due to the appalling violence
Set upon the Israeli atheletes
In the Olympic village

May the bravery of those participants
Embolden our hearts always

—Mogen David

Forgiveness

Forgiveness
Getting to a place where you decide to let it all ride[5]
What sticks in the throat…
The swallowing of pride
To be within earshot of a braggadocious tongue
God's admonition of his chosen ones
You dance while I have to smite my Egyptian children

Forgiveness
The power of forgiveness
Is in understanding the nature of the beast
Tooth and claw
Human maw
How do those who have the most
Cater to those who have the least?

The rest is commentary

---

5. 1982, Tom Petty and the Heartbreakers "Deliver Me". *Long After Dark.* Backstreet Records

Busy Murals Finale

Wanna know how to beat any funk?

Ya gotta do every last thing that enters your mind

Get up and put the soap in the bath as it fills

It's better that way

Get up and floss

Get up and fold those clothes that have been sitting on the
    foot of the bed for a week

Get up and clean the fridge

The microwave is … growing

The commode!

The mirror is no such thing

The ashtray's a volleyball

Get up and paint over the scrawled message you and
    Courtney inscribed on the wall

With magnum sharpie some time ago

Clean your telephone screen

It's … *bacon*

Clip your nails

God!

The air-conditioner filter is froth

The sink has influenza

Change your art around

You'll be glad you did

And call your mother!

And wash your feet before bathing, dude

No ... fucking *wash* them
The kitchen garbage has erupted
Again!

Get up!
Do something for yourself
Let the cat out!

Is there any smoked Gouda left?

—Maiche Lev with D.B., September, 2020

Other Books by Maiche Lev

Speaking Circus

Lights Down

Floored

Still Life - With Extras

Deadlock Backdraft: Above the Elecric Gardens

On the Moon You Sharpen Stone

Deliverance

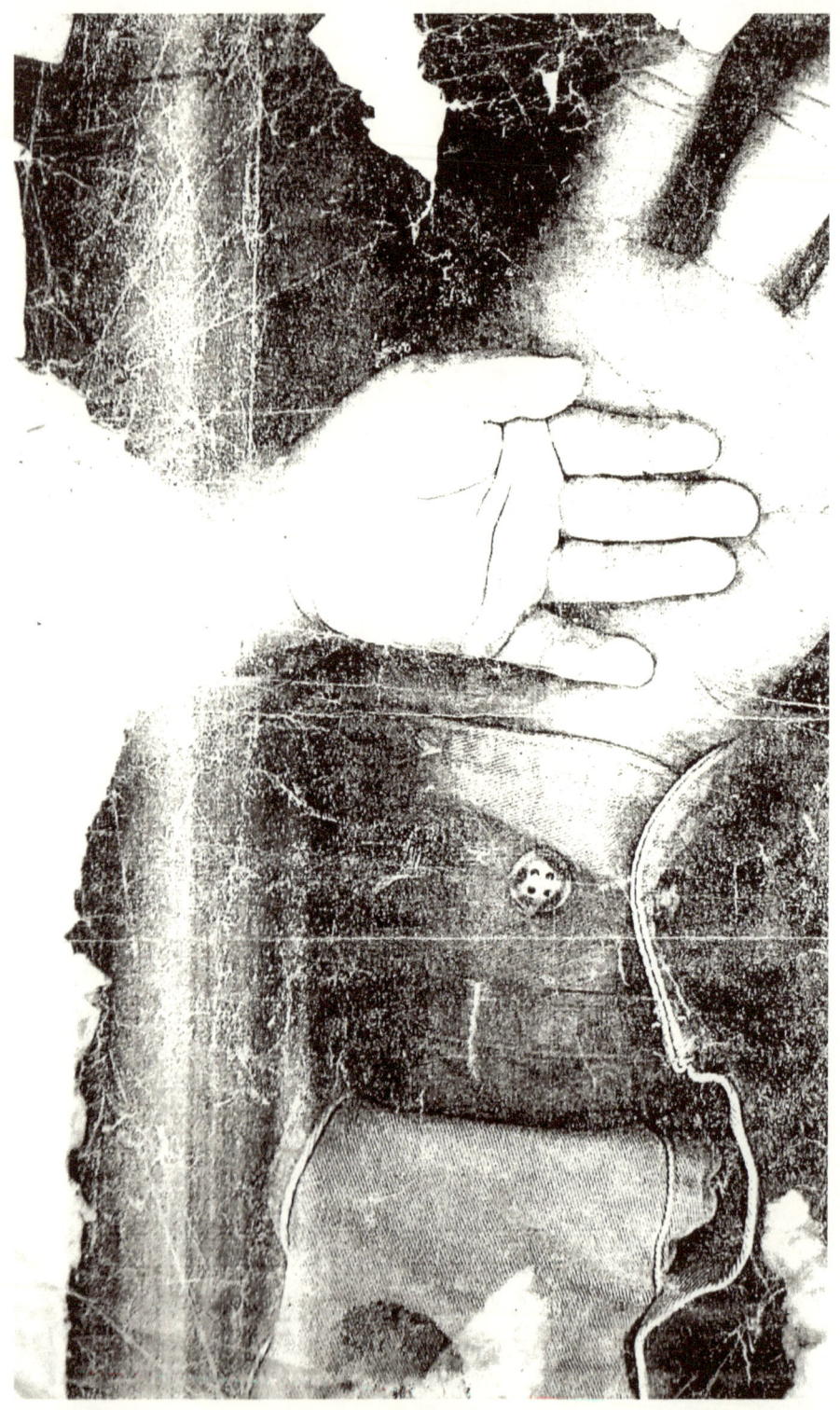